WORK WITHOUT FEAR

How to get over the fears that are holding you back

Written by Coralie Closon
Translated by Rebecca Neal

FURTHER READING 31

IS FREEDOM FROM FEAR POSSIBLE?

- **Issue:** is it possible to definitively free ourselves from our fears in order to be more effective and feel more comfortable at work?
- **Uses:** gaining control over your anxieties and no longer letting them run your life: this is the key to progressing smoothly, with full power over yourself and your abilities in your professional environment.
- **Professional context:** professional relationships, job changes, work-related uncertainty, interviews, public speaking, work-life balance.
- **FAQs:**
  - I am constantly anxious before I go into the office, but I don't know why. How can I overcome this fear?
  - I no longer find meaning in what I do, and this situation paralyses me and gives me anxiety. How can I get out of it?
  - When I am supposed to speak in front of a group of people, I am overwhelmed by fear. What can I do to overcome this stress?
  - When I am in front of my boss, my behaviour completely changes, I become restless and I lose control of myself. Why?
  - I would like to change my working hours, but I don't dare talk about it. How can I start?
  - My company has just been bought out and I am afraid for the future. How can I deal with this situation?
  - In the short term, what tools could help me to manage the physical symptoms caused by anxiety?

Nowadays, society and the world of work are always asking us to deliver more, more quickly: performance is what counts. Our relationships with our colleagues and our managers, as well as our private lives, are experiencing the same pressure. We have less time to communicate, listen to each other and understand each other. This climate gives rise to fears which, fortunately, can be overcome if we start by identifying and accepting them in order to then understand them. Although fear is a normal feeling in certain unfamiliar situations, this emotion can be extremely paralysing if we have no control over it.

Imagine the following situations: it is finally time to present the project you have been working on for weeks, but your hands are clammy, you are finding it difficult to breathe, your heart rate is rising, and no sound is coming from your lips; after a comment from your manager, you have a lump in your throat and you cannot answer them; you need to change your working hours to find better balance, but you don't dare to speak to your manager about it. These unpleasant moments are often part of all of our day-to-day lives.

However, when we let this kind of situation become a reflex, we risk getting bogged down and lost in it. Anxiety can inhibit our actions and reactions when confronting a situation or person that makes us anxious. Our creativity, our initiative and our assertiveness decrease and we feel stuck, unable to be who we really are. In theory, we could get around the problem by remaining in a secure, familiar and risk-free place. However, this comfort zone will never allow us to thrive; quite the opposite, in fact. This does not even take into account the fact that reality will end up catching up with us. In this case, there is only one solution: face the situation head on!

WORKING WITHOUT FEAR: THE BASICS

UNDERSTANDING YOUR FEAR

A basic emotion

Fear, which is defined by the Collins English Dictionary as "a feeling of distress, apprehension, or alarm caused by impending danger, pain, etc", is appropriate when it protects us from a real threat. In such cases, it is an instinctive reaction which becomes an effective defence mechanism in a dangerous situation. However, it can also come from our imaginations and be nothing more than the projection of a potential threat. In the world of work, it is normally this second case that we come across. Consequently, we must interpret the scenarios that we come up with in our minds to see whether they are well-founded.

According to Paul Ekman (American psychologist, born in 1934) fear is one of the four fundamental emotions, along with happiness, sadness and anger. It is therefore natural to feel it. What is less natural, however, is creating a discrepancy between our reactions and the emotions we feel. Pierre-Jean de Jonghe (coach and president of the Leading and Coaching Academy in Belgium) describes three ways of doing this:

- **Stifling emotion,** which is an avoidance strategy ("I don't want to accept what I am feeling, so I won't express it").
- **Exaggerating emotion,** which indicates a lack of self-

control ("I shout at my employees even when I am not angry").

- **Substitution,** which involves expressing a different feeling to the one that is felt. This is known as an 'extorting' emotion. This is the case, for example, when we laugh because we are uncomfortable or afraid (nervous laughter).

It is therefore important to picture our way of reacting when fear emerges. Is it appropriate for the situation we are experiencing?

Identifying your fear

The first stage in getting rid of anxiety is admitting that it exists. After that, we can start to identify where it comes from and why, and what we can do to overcome it. This long road must be travelled with a real will to change if you want to successfully pull yourself out of the mire.

Whether you fear expressing yourself in front of your manager, failing, coming into conflict with someone, setting boundaries, speaking in public or a range of other things, fears are always linked to an individual's experience and can seriously hold them back in their day-to-day lives. These anxious thoughts often say something about us and our needs: for example, behind a fear of conflict we often find a need for emotional security. In the professional world, we can distinguish three main types of fears: social judgement, failure and uncertainty. To try to conquer them, we must start by understanding them better.

UNDERSTANDING THEIR ORIGINS

Drivers

In transactional analysis, the American psychologist Taibi Kahler (born in 1943) has identified five 'drivers'. These messages form guidelines inherited from our parents and our upbringing which lead to our reactions and make us adopt unconscious behaviour in a particular situation. This causes problems when these attitudes are inappropriate and hinder our progress. Fears can then take root and interfere with authentic behaviour.

A description of each of these drivers will allow you to recognise these mechanisms at work in you and in others, in order to know yourself better and understand other people better. You can leave judgement aside and become more tolerant towards yourself and others. Keep firmly in mind that these tools and methods of analysis are still very simplified: each person is unique and can be guided by several drivers with varying degrees of dominance:

- **Be perfect:** when excellence is demanded throughout childhood, when failure is not tolerated and effort is not emphasised, the adult will probably tend towards obsessive perfectionism. If you are in this situation, you are stressed and inflexible towards yourself and others. In short, you are perennially dissatisfied. The fear linked to this pressure is the fear of not being accepted in society or liked by others if you are not perfect.
- **Be strong:** this driver reflects a strict upbringing in which there is not always room for feelings and emotions.

Individuality is favoured. Confiding in others is seen as a sign of weakness. A person affected by this driver is generally disciplined and remains cold in the face of other people's emotions. They are afraid of showing their own emotions, and they will tend to avoid situations which could put them in danger – meaning situations which would force them to confront their emotions and therefore expose their weaknesses.

- **Hurry up:** "Come on son, we're going to be late!" Since childhood, this person has had to rush to go to school, take their bath, eat, etc. If this driver is dominant for you, you are often late, you are always rushing everywhere, and your diary is filled to bursting. Subconsciously, you are seeking the stress of time flying by in order to perform. You no doubt believe that the more overbooked you are, the more efficient you will be. But beware, as fatigue risks prevailing and anxiety may emerge when calm returns.

- **Please others:** this driver affects the child who has learnt by being told "finish your dinner and make Mummy happy" that in order to be recognised, they must please adults. Once they themselves become adults, they will prioritise the happiness and needs of other people to the detriment of their own. Helping people will make them feel alive, and it will become difficult for them to say no. The individual who follows this pattern has only one fear: of no longer being loved if they do not do what is asked of them. If you recognise yourself in this, take care that you do not let yourself be exploited.

- **Try hard:** with this kind of message, life appears as a permanent struggle. Here, the information received by the child puts the emphasis on effort rather than on the results themselves. Fear arises when they cannot try any harder or when they think that others are not trying hard enough. It can turn into fear of failure, of ease or even of success.

Now that you have a clearer picture of these drivers, position yourself as an objective observer of your situation (this is called the meta-position). Take time to reflect on your habits, your obsessions, your attitudes in professional relationships, the kind of upbringing you give to your children, etc.

You will find a brief self-coaching exercise in the 'Over to you' section. It will allow you to analyse yourself in order to highlight your drivers and the various behaviours linked to them. Try to always be objective and put things into perspective as much as possible. For example, if you cannot say no to your boss or even to your employees, ask yourself whether this behaviour is really justified or whether it is an expression of your driver. If you are regularly late and calm makes you anxious, were you aware that this could be a result of a repeated pattern in your environment? Finally, are the behaviours that you inherited during your childhood still in place today?

In transactional analysis, there are five 'permissions' which could help you to knock down your drivers. Try to put them into practice every day. Each person has their own technique – you could repeat them out loud, sing them, write them on a Post-it note or a board, etc.

Driver	Permission
Be perfect	Be as you are. You have the right to make mistakes. Perfection does not exist.
Be strong	Be open. You have the right to feel and express emotions.
Hurry up	Take your time. Adopt an effective and appropriate pace. It is no use rushing and risking doing things badly.
Please others	Please yourself. Live according to your own values and take care of yourself.
Try hard	Set your own limits and your own goals, but do not do too much: excessive tiredness will not help you.

WARNING

If you do not manage to feel something positive by stating your permission and you feel uneasy instead, there is probably another heavier, deeper element in your history that is stopping you from making progress. In this case, do not hesitate to get help from someone else.

Drivers therefore have a negative effect on behaviour and can lead to unjustified fears and anxieties which involve the judgement of the self or others in relation to the self. They are the origin of our limiting beliefs (cf. following section), which themselves are the root of our fears and anxious thoughts.

Be careful: the aim is never to completely eradicate a behaviour, but to preserve and highlight the positive elements it could bring to a certain situation and alter the rest. Here are some examples of the 'qualities in our faults' with regard to drivers:

- the 'Be perfect' is produces high-quality work;
- the 'Be strong' is resistant to high-stress and high-pressure situations, and knows how to handle a crisis;
- the 'Hurry up' is very responsive and can meet very short deadlines;
- the 'Please others' is good company and empathetic;
- the 'Try hard' is patient and persistent.

Beliefs

Drivers lead us to beliefs. Most of the time, our fears are linked to these. From birth, our experiences and environment lead us to generate 'beliefs' which are grounded in our subconscious. They involve all the conclusions we have come to with regard to our lived experiences, including those dictated by our drivers. Together, they form our vision of the world, our certainties and our fears. They dictate our behaviour, the way we react to situations and our opinions, and they do all this without us being aware of it. They are strong and difficult to get rid of. We tend to protect them so that our vision of the world will remain coherent.

There are two kinds of belief, known as limiting beliefs and supporting beliefs:

- Supporting beliefs are positive ("I can do it"), as they give us energy, motivate us to take action, and give us permissions and confidence.

- Limiting beliefs move us away from action. They form a view of life that makes us think that we do not deserve certain things or that we cannot achieve them. They place a veil over reality, and can lead to real anxieties. For example, if we are convinced that we do not deserve a promotion, we will subconsciously do everything possible to make this belief come true.

What interests us here is learning how to move past the limiting beliefs that are at the root of our fears and anxious thoughts. In coaching, the basic tool is reframing through questioning. The aim is to adopt another point of view on the situation and another perception of what we thought was certain in our reality. To do this, it is necessary to keep a very open mind and to have a sincere desire or need to change. You will need to destroy conclusions that have been reached throughout your entire life and 'clear your formatting' so that you can be reprogrammed. To do this, question how well-founded all your certainties are and find examples from your life which disprove them (you can use The Work of Byron Katie to help you, cf. 'Over to you'). Look again and again, because the more arguments you have against this certainty, the quicker it will collapse. Next, take action to help your new positive beliefs take root, cultivate them and test them from day to day so that they gradually become part of you and your daily life.

Needs

Neuroscience confirms that it is useless to tell yourself to stop being scared. First we must return to our beliefs, needs and emotions so that we can understand our anxiety and then treat it. Many people will try to conceal their fear. They will put all their energy into this, even if it means exhausting themselves and reaching the point of burnout. It is therefore very important not to try to bury your anxiety, but to talk about it in order to free yourself from it.

To know if your motivation to change – in this case the motivation to control your fears – is strong enough, you need to discover the unsatisfied need hidden behind your fears. The more important this need is for you, the more it will drive you.

To help you in this process, Maslow's hierarchy of needs represents the different needs we could have. It organises these needs into five levels, ranked by order of importance. According to Abraham Maslow (American psychologist, 1908-1970), all these needs are present in all of us, but some of them are felt more than others. His idea is that we cannot act on our higher motivations if our lower motivations are not satisfied.

Try to identify the needs you are most sensitive to and which could fuel your anxiety. For example, if your need for esteem is not respected in a particular situation, realising this will increase your motivation to act.

WORKING ON YOURSELF

The ego states

We have just looked at where our fears could come from. In this section, we will move on to looking at what part of us is responsible for these fears. This will allow us to challenge the consistency of our anxieties and give us material to question.

Eric Berne (American psychiatrist, 1910-1970), the father of transactional analysis, outlined three internal states of a person at a given moment facing a particular situation. He intellectualised them to enable us to better interpret them. They can therefore be viewed as tools of behavioural and developmental analysis which evoke what is happening within us.

The ego states

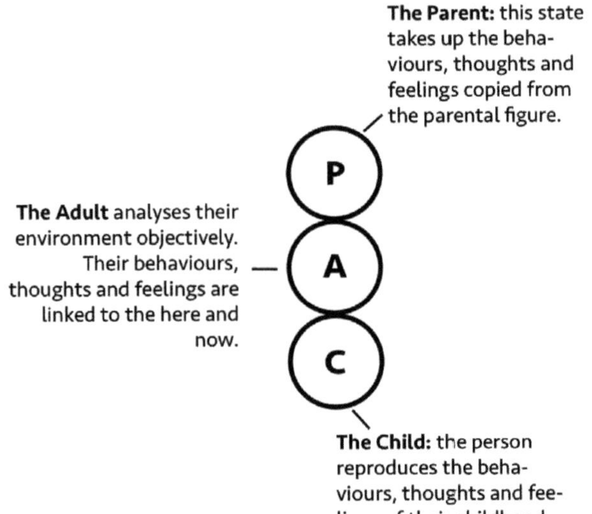

Try to put your finger on moments in your life when you act like you did when you were a child, and those when you adopt behaviour copied from those older than you. If you cannot identify them in this way, simply think of times when you reacted immediately, and try to understand what could have influenced your reaction. Say, for example, you break out in a cold sweat at the thought of speaking in public. Who is behind this fear? Often, you will find the Child, and becoming aware of that will allow you to take the first step towards change. How would you act if the Adult took over the reins, and what needs to happen for this to be the case? What resources are at your disposal?

In order to be balanced, we all need these three states. The Adult allows us to react appropriately to an immediate situation, the Child gives us our touch of madness and our spontaneity, and the Parent brings us the rules of society. Each state provides us with several resources:

- the Parent brings values, beliefs, rules and opinions;
- the Child brings emotions, intuition and curiosity;
- the Adult brings logic, information and objective analysis.

What is also interesting is that these states influence our relationships. The transactions between two people are simple when they are both in the Adult state, but this is not always the case. Fears can result from a communication problem. It is therefore important to clarify transactions between the participants in a stressful situation.

The three possible transactions

- The transaction can be **parallel or complementary** when the response is appropriate. It only involves two ego states: one per person. For example, you take the Child position with your boss and your boss respond to you as a Parent. Communication works.
- The transaction can be **crossed.** For example, your boss talks to you as an Adult and you react as a Child, no doubt because the situation brings back a memory for you. Communication is broken.

- **Ulterior or hidden** transactions also take place on the psychological level: as well as the verbal message, there is a nonverbal message. This second-level transaction is hidden and often takes place subconsciously. For example, your boss asks you what time it is when the meeting should be starting right this minute. You take this as a reproach and although you respond verbally to them as an Adult, on the inside you feel bad and your gestures and tone of voice respond as a Child. Communication is broken.

The three transactions

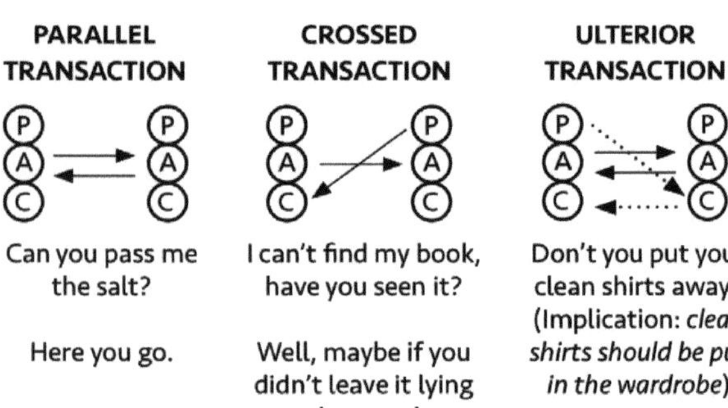

It is therefore important to constantly question yourself to try and understand why communication is not working.

These ego states are useful as a tool for analysing the situation, but also as a source of motivation to change when you become aware of them. If, for example, you no longer find meaning in your work, ask yourself who thinks that: is it the Child with broken dreams? What were their dreams? What does the Adult want? Can you find balance in order to regain your peace of mind? To use an interpersonal example, let's say you are afraid of responding to your manager or to a colleague: what is holding you back at that time? Why? What feelings does the other person inspire in you? What position are they in at those times? What could you put in place to get things moving?

Moving past your fears will happen thanks to detailed self-questioning about the situation. Always keep an open mind and be as objective as possible. Theory is only there to get you thinking.

TOP TIPS

- Take time to understand and analyse the situation and all the participants who play a part in it. Particularly for those whose dominant driver is 'hurry up', do not rush to judgements or conclusions. Nothing is black and white and we are all partly responsible for what happens to us. Becoming aware of our responsibility is the first step towards change. If you are afraid of going to the office, it is not necessarily because your boss is bullying you. Mental shortcuts are often one of the main reasons we remain imprisoned by fear.
- When you have the situation that is causing you problems in mind, try to set yourself a clear and realistic goal to gradually overcome your fear. Formulate it in a positive way and make a to-do list to gradually overcome your fear. You should also draw up a list of your internal resources and of the people around you who could help you.
- Never lose sight of your needs. If they are not respected as you move towards change, you will not get there.
- Action prevents procrastination, and the more you let your fear confine you, the more it will control your life. Get started as quickly as possible. As action leads to more action, you will soon feel that you are an agent of change and your level of motivation will only be higher.
- If you are totally lost regarding your place in your company or if your anxiety is only on the level of communication between you and your colleagues, you can use 360-degree feedback. This involves drawing up a list of

questions about yourself for the people at your company and asking them for their feedback. These questions could include, for example: what am I like as a manager? What are my qualities and what are my flaws as a leader? How could I improve? etc. Opening up the lines of communication is often a source of general wellbeing. Even if not all of it is easy to hear, it is an excellent approach to gain a new outlook on a situation which has stalled. You must be prepared to accept criticism, but also compliments.

- Never remain alone with your fear: always try to find somebody to share your worries with, whether they are a friend, a colleague, a family member or a professional coach. Talking about your fears makes them less frightening.
- If you are particularly affected by one of the subjects broached, feel free to gather information to tackle it in more depth. Each person has their own tendencies, and no tool can work for everybody. You must find your own formula for freeing yourself from the causes of your anxiety.
- Never let fear completely overwhelm you and paralyse you. As soon as it rears its head, stop it using an anchor point (see 'FAQs' section), breathing techniques, meditation, etc.
- Try to remain positive whatever happens. There is nothing worse than letting dark ideas overwhelm you so that you turn in on yourself and avoid confronting your fear. Use the Coué method, for example, by repeating to yourself that you can do it.

THE COUÉ METHOD

At the end of the 19th century, Émile Coué de la Châtaigneraie (French psychologist and pharmacist, 1857-1926) gradually developed his method, which is based on self-hypnosis and autosuggestion. The idea is that we can act on our subconscious through our imagination: by altering our mental representations, we can move our subconscious, and consequently our health, our behaviour, our actions, etc. in a positive direction.

- As part of your process, regularly use self-questioning and meta-positioning, as these will allow you to remain objective and broaden your outlook on the situation.
- When the entire questioning process is over and you have a clear aim, carry out more and more small gestures and acts of courage to strengthen your new drive. Do not rest on your laurels after small victories.

FAQS

I AM CONSTANTLY ANXIOUS BEFORE I GO INTO THE OFFICE, BUT I DON'T KNOW WHY. HOW CAN I OVERCOME THIS FEAR?

You have already accepted that you have a problem – well done! Now, you need to investigate the origin of your fear. How does your anxiety manifest itself and at what precise moment does it appear? When you sense it coming on, stop there, feel it and question it before you go into your office. Close your eyes: what are its symptoms? What triggers them? Is it justified? Once you have identified the reason, you can work on your fear in order to move past it.

I NO LONGER FIND MEANING IN WHAT I DO, AND THIS SITUATION PARALYSES ME AND GIVES ME ANXIETY. HOW CAN I GET OUT OF IT?

Are you disappointed by your work? Are you unable to see where it is going to lead you? Are you becoming critical towards your colleagues, and especially those who are dealing well with this situation? Do you feel that you do not know how to get out of this quicksand? In this case, the origin of your fear seems to run deep and you should certainly think about taking part in a coaching session with a professional to redefine your needs and values, in order to find a degree of peace of mind in the long run.

WHEN I AM SUPPOSED TO SPEAK IN FRONT OF A GROUP OF PEOPLE, I AM OVERWHELMED BY FEAR. WHAT CAN I DO TO OVERCOME THIS STRESS?

In this case, you could be hampered by a limiting belief, by a little voice that whispers in your ear that you can't do it. Do not let your subconscious dictate your life. Can you bring back a memory of a time when public speaking went well for you? What does "can't do it" mean to you? What is the feedback on your presentations like?

In this case, the SCORE model (which you will find in the 'Over to you' section) may help you.

WHEN I AM IN FRONT OF MY BOSS, MY BEHAVIOUR COMPLETELY CHANGES, I BECOME RESTLESS AND I LOSE CONTROL OF MYSELF. WHY?

Start by analysing the root of this discomfort: what attitudes from your boss cause it? Try to put your finger on the emotions you feel: fear, anger, sadness? Are they justified? Often, your objective answer to this will be no. Then ask yourself if they remind you of anyone. Here, there is a chance that you will find the image of another person who you have associated with your boss or simply with the position that they occupy. Realising this is the first step; now you must try to work on this association.

For example, if you act as a Child (cf. 'The ego states') in front of a boss who reminds you of your father, who you have a difficult relationship with, change this association through questioning and reframing. Are they the same? Is the relationship the same? Is adopting this ego state justified? See what you can put in place to make the situation progress: talk to your boss or your father about it, adopt a different attitude now that you have become aware of it, etc.

I WOULD LIKE TO CHANGE MY WORKING HOURS, BUT I DON'T DARE TALK ABOUT IT. HOW CAN I START?

You don't dare to say no to a meeting, which reduces your time for yourself and increases your stress levels. First of all, ask yourself what would happen if you dared to talk about it. What are your fears and the real risks that you are running? Are all your colleagues in the same boat? Then, clearly identify what you need: this will give you the motivation to reach your goal. Finally, ask yourself what concrete actions you can undertake, such as buying yourself another phone for personal use, sending an email to indicate when you can be contacted, talking to your manager, etc. You can use the SCORE model to help you achieve your goal (cf. 'Over to you').

MY COMPANY HAS JUST BEEN BOUGHT OUT AND I AM AFRAID FOR THE FUTURE. HOW CAN I DEAL WITH THIS SITUATION?

What are you really afraid of? Is it losing your identity, losing your job, change in general? Is this fear in line with the reality? To help you to put the situation into perspective and see it more clearly, use self-questioning about anxious thoughts (in the 'Over to you' section). Once your outlook is more objective, you can work on your goals and how to reach them (see the SCORE model in the 'Over to you' section).

IN THE SHORT TERM, WHAT TOOLS COULD HELP ME TO MANAGE THE PHYSICAL SYMPTOMS CAUSED BY ANXIETY?

Using anchor points is a method which allows you to draw on a personal resource whenever you want. It is easy to use and can be useful in situations where you feel uncomfortable. It works as follows:

- Choose and internal resource that you possess, such as "I write very well".
- Associate it with an event from the past which is in your memory, such as the pride you felt the first time you received a good mark for an essay at school.
- Close your eyes and relive that experience as if you were there. Associate what you are feeling with a gesture such as a clenched fist, a hand on your stomach, crossed fingers, etc. Repeat at least three times, reliving the

experience each time.

- Check that the gesture you have chosen is fully associated with this internal resource.
- Now it is over to you: make use of this gesture whenever you need it.

GOOD TO KNOW

The more you use the anchor point, the more beneficial it will be. Conversely, it will become less effective if you leave it on the shelf.

OVER TO YOU

DISCOVER YOUR DRIVERS

Fill in the table below to identify your dominant drivers and their consequences for you.

In the first column, write down how much you think you are affected by each of these drivers on a scale from 1 (least affected) to 10 (most affected). Secondly, give concrete examples of the way that they manifest themselves in you. Thirdly, note their disadvantages, the things that harm your relationships, the things that affect the way you see yourself, etc. Next, list the advantages of each driver. Finally, try to identify what action you could take in order to find a balance which leverages the advantages while eliminating the disadvantages as much as possible.

	Degree	Manifestations	Disadvantages	Advantages	Balance
Be perfect					
Be strong					
Hurry up					
Please others					
Try hard					

This little test will allow you to better understand your behaviour and its origins. Once you have zoomed in on the different drivers that inhabit you, you can finally see whether your feelings and actions are appropriate or not. This understanding will reinforce your will to change when you need it the most. The permissions then become all the more powerful.

SELF-QUESTIONING ON ANXIOUS THOUGHTS

The more you try to deny your fears, the more you will increase your anxiety in the long term. The immediate feeling of relief after you avoid them is only an illusion which will soon be replaced by profound anxiety. We have seen that self-questioning is a powerful weapon to confront your anxious thoughts. Here are some relevant questions taken from Christophe André's book *Guide de psychologie de la vie quotidienne* ['Guide to psychology in everyday life']:

- Am I sure that the thing I am afraid of will happen? What arguments do I have to say that my thought is correct?
- What is the worst thing that could happen to me?
- Have I already encountered similar situations in the past? Were my predictions correct? Did they come true?
- What do the statistics say on this subject?
- What would a person who is not afraid of this situation say?
- If my thought does come true, what can I do?

These questions aim to make you adopt a more realistic

vision of your fear, based on facts rather than beliefs.

'THE WORK OF BYRON KATIE'

The fear that we feel is not always justified. Consequently, to get rid of it we should correctly analyse the situation. The Work is a simple but powerful method of personal questioning. It aims to attain happiness by challenging the thoughts that are at the root of our suffering. As soon as you are facing a stressful thought, ask yourself the four questions below:

- Is it true?
- Can you absolutely know that it's true?
- How do you react - what happens - when you believe that thought?
- Who would you be without the thought?

Reframe the thought in different ways (for example, "He never listens to me" can become "He always listens to me", "I never listen to him", "He sometimes listens to me", etc.), then find at least three good reasons why each reframing is just as true as, and perhaps even truer than, the initial statement. The goal of this method is to give us a jolt in order to erode our certainties. Give it a try!

THE SCORE MODEL

Created by Robert Dilts, a consultant and trainer in the field of neuro-linguistic programming, this model enables you to overcome obstacles in order to achieve your goal. This model can be used in almost all situations, provided that there is a clear aim and an obstacle has been identified. In our case, the obstacle would be the fear and anxiety generated by a situation.

For example, you are afraid of public speaking (obstacle), but you have to lead a meeting in front of a group of people (aim). Identify the five points of this model to overcome the fears that are stopping you from progressing.

The SCORE model

Problem	
Symptoms	These are all the visible elements of the problem, the way you feel.
Causes	The things that fuel the symptoms.

Solution	
Aims	This is the desired state which would replace the symptoms.
Resources	These are all the internal and external resources that would allow the aim/desired state to be reached (training, relationships, strong points, etc.).
Effects	These are the long-term results (qualitative and/or quantitative).

We want to hear from you!
Leave a comment on your online library
and share your favourite books on social media!

FURTHER READING

BIBLIOGRAPHY

- André, C. (2008) *Le guide de psychologie de la vie quotidienne*. Paris: Odile Jacob.
- Auger, L. (2004) *S'aider soi-même, une psychothérapie par la raison*. Montreal: Éditions de l'Homme.
- Cannio, S. and Launer, V. (2014) *Cas de coaching commentés*. Paris: Éditions d'Organisation.
- Closon, J. (2012) *Maladresses Parentales, s'en sortir et ne pas reproduire*. Belgium: ITEP Éditions.
- D' Ansembourg, T. (2007) *Being Genuine: Stop Being Nice, Start Being Real*. California: Puddle Dancer Press.
- De Jonghe, P.-J. (2004) *De quelle vie voulez-vous être le héros ? Tirer profit du passé pour réorganiser sa vie*. Paris: InterÉditions.
- Pascual, S. (No date) Connaissance de soi: Les messages contraignants. *Ithaque Coaching*. [Online]. [Accessed 10 November 2016]. Available from: <http://www. ithaquecoaching.com/articles/connaissance-de-soi-les-messages-contraignants-1577.html>
- Stewart, I. and Joines, V. (2012) *T A Today: A New Introduction to Transactional Analysis*. North Carolina: Lifespace Publishing.

ADDITIONAL SOURCES

- Damasio, A. (2006) *Descartes' Error: Emotion, Reason and the Human Brain*. London: Vintage.
- Kahler, T. (1975) Drivers: The Key to the Process Script.

Transactional Analysis Journal, 5(3), pp. 280-284.
- Kaher, T. (2008) *The Process Therapy Model: The Six Personality Types with Adaptations*. United Staes of America: Kahler Communications, Inc.
- Goleman, D. (1996) *Emotional Intelligence: Why It Can Matter More Than IQ*. London: Bloomsbury.
- Goleman, D. (1999) *Working With Emotional Intelligence*. New York: Bantam Dell.
- Steiner, C. (2003) *Emotional Literacy: Intelligence With a Heart*. California, Personhood Press.